EMBODYING MOVEMENT™

Ground your whole being.

Restore balance in your life. Discover how to embrace
your whole being through the life-enhancing benefits of body movement.

EMBODYING MOVEMENT COPYRIGHT

Please note:

The written or spoken information, ideas, procedures and suggestions contained and presented in 'EMBODYING MOVEMENT' workshops and books are meant for educational purposes only and are not for diagnosis. It should not be used as a substitute for your physician's advice. 'EMBODYING MOVEMENT' is not therapy and is not intended to replace the recommendations of a licensed health practitioner. It is the responsibility of the reader to consult with his or her own medical Doctor, Counselor, Therapist or other competent professional regarding any condition before adopting any of the suggestions in this book.

EMBODYING MOVEMENT™

*Dedicated to the graceful inner strength
of the body, which fully supports our journey
to be of service to our life's calling.*

MISSION STATEMENT

To guide and facilitate women
in becoming their most beautiful and radiant selves.

To acknowledge and embrace the well of love
and power which lies within all women and to ignite the
awakening and embodying of this life force.

To empower each woman, through exquisite self-care and love,
to live her fullest life possible, and to walk her path of wisdom
and truth, as she shares this light and knowledge
with all beings.

IN DEEP GRATITUDE
Thank you

The creation, birth and life of 'A Woman's Truth' would not have been possible without the love, support and devotion from the following angels in my life:

My beautiful daughter Megan who naturally embodies the teachings of living in her truth and integrity, thank you for the creative gift of the beautiful artwork. Helena Nelson-Reed for her generosity of spirit in allowing her extraordinary artwork, which embodies the teachings so magnificently, to grace the covers. Dennise Marie Keller for her unwavering support and dedication to the teachings and for proofing, editing, aligning and translating my vision into the technical world of manifestation. Dan Fowler for his creative genius and dedication. Lucy Alexander and Suzanne Ryan, my dearest friends for their amazing editing and wholehearted encouragement. Monica Marsh for her commitment, support and belief in the workshops. Maggie Crawford, my mum, for her proofing and for being a living example of the teachings. Cait Myer and Katie Steen for their patience and ability to decipher my handwriting and for formatting the books. Bethany Kelly for her support. Deborah Waring for holding the space for the conception of 'A Woman's Truth' to be born and for her insight in the first year of teaching and Emmanuel for believing in my vision.

My mentors and teachers Rod Stryker, Adyashanti and Alison Armstrong, Max Simon and Jeffrey Van Dyk for their continuous and guiding light in my life, their never-ending belief in my potential and for always teaching me the way to evolve into my highest and most potent self. And to all of you beautiful and courageous women who are committing to living your truth and transforming into your most radiant selves,

thank you.

A PRELUDE

An overture to embodying movement.

*"Our body holds the pathway to our feminine expression.
By opening to our free flowing movement, we connect to the natural rhythm
of the body. Movement is an effortless way to access our body wisdom,
open up to deep healing, and connect to our Divine feminine energy source."*

As a child and teenager, growing up movement was part of my life. While I continued to exercise to "keep fit" it was not until I went to a movement class when I was in my late 30's that I fell in love with moving my body! I went to an authentic movement class where I was able to really feel my body and get to know myself in a very different way. This came at a time of my exploration of understanding my worth as a woman and discovering the feminine side of me.

Movement is key in the ownership and understanding of our body, to our relationship to ourselves, because movement brings us into our body, it is a body centered experience. For me moving my body is a kind of spiritual experience as it brings me into connection with my breath, with nature, the earth, and brings me into the present moment.

Miranda brings such insight into how to bring movement into your life, and the importance of it in regards to living your full potential and feeling your worth as woman. I encourage you to enjoy your body by finding the movement that works for you. I found mine.

What is the movement that stirs your soul?

~ Tarnie Fulloon, PT
Creator of BodyFreedom

Our bodies are in constant motion. From long before our first breath to our last, from the subtle movement within our cells, to the intricate use of our fingers, toes and tongue, to the broad and sweeping gestures of our limbs, we function and communicate through movement. Indeed, it is the continual ebb and flow within our organs – the movement of our heart and lungs – that keeps us alive.

However, it is not enough. To thrive in and make optimal use of our body-temples we must bring conscious awareness to our inner and outer motion, and add intentional movement in the form of appropriate exercise or dance.

That is where this book comes in. In these pages, Miranda beautifully explains the holistic benefits of conscious movement and the gentle and loving ways in which each of us can incorporate more of it into our daily lives. Through her thoughtful, inspiring, and practical words, she guides and encourages us to make choices that bring us greater health and vitality, and reduce stress. For seasoned movers and aspiring beginners alike there is much of value in the teachings in "Embodying Movement."

Miranda knows of what she speaks. She is a living example of the thriving life force she describes in her book. I encourage you to take to heart her invitation to become a better steward of your body through movement.

~ Leah Leddy
RPP, Movement Facilitator Simple Ordinary Presence

EMBODYING MOVEMENT™

Gems of Truth

Download a copy of the **Embodying Movement Study**

from Miranda's website at:

www.MirandaJBarrett.com/resources/embodying-movement

A DAILY PRACTICE

commit to Yourself

*F*ollow these simple steps daily as a way to instill and strengthen your heartfelt resolve to love yourself. This will help to keep you aligned, transforming and on track, giving you a stable foundation for the rest of your life. As a gift to yourself, please mark the teachings as you read them through and congratulate yourself with each one. See each day as a commitment to take exquisite care of yourself.

Download a copy of the **Embodying Movement Study**

from Miranda's website at:

www.MirandaJBarrett.com/resources/embodying-movement

A LIFE WORTH LIVING

"Never give from your well.
Always give from your overflow."

~ Rumi

All too often as women, your own needs are denied for the benefit of others as you orchestrate your life through demands and expectations you feel responsible for. Unfortunately, this can leave you without the juice and energy needed to be present fully and to enjoy life. During these readings, you will continually discover more about who you truly are and learn the tools needed to live your most authentic and fulfilling life possible. From this place, you will experience being 'full to overflowing' and all the joy and energy this brings.

As you delve into these teachings, you will explore, laugh, study, share, and freely express who you are. In this sacred space, you will ultimately learn your truth as a woman in order to shine, to embody your own beauty, believe in your own worth, and take exquisite care of yourself. For only in this way can you truly be of service.

During these guidebooks, many of the basic needs of women will be explored such as sleep, nutrition, creativity, movement and time to replenish. A topic has been chosen for each book and a cohesive and practical foundation is laid out to inspire and guide you. This will bring about a new strength and resolve which will allow your needs to become a priority, without letting your outer world dictate otherwise. By the end of our time together, the concept of being confident, loving, serene and passionate will no longer be a distant fantasy. Instead, these and many other extraordinary qualities that you naturally embody as a woman will flow with ease, grace and love.

With life's demands so high, it has become imperative that your needs are first acknowledged, honored and then taken care of. From this vantage point, your relationship with yourself then has the potential to be transformed into one of self-love. The beauty is this in turn creates a life that not only fulfills you and your life's purpose, but also allows everyone touched by your presence to receive this gift.

I look forward to spending this precious time with you.

Welcome to A Woman's Truth.

Sincerely and with love,

Miranda

EMBODYING MOVEMENT

Our bodies are our temples.
The sanctuary in which we live.
The vessel through which we express who we are.

When you are well and healthy, life force and vitality pours through you. It does not matter how you are dressed or even what you are doing, this vibrant energy is palpable, even magnetic. This vigor is often why you are attracted to someone.

In this world, where stress has become a constant companion, it can be challenging to keep vitality alive. It is well known that stress is a number one player in exhausting your energy supply and can even distort how you look. Your jaw line tightens, your lips thin, your shoulders hunch and energy can no longer flow through you.

Gone are the times when moving your body was as natural as the day's rhythm. Chopping wood, carrying water, farming the land, washing, and walking were activities that kept the body lean, flexible, and strong.

Yet in modern times, what is demanded of the mind is now valued more highly than what is asked of the body. It seems as though convenience and stimulation have taken over. Even to the point where there has to be a conscious choice made to maintain a healthy sleep rhythm due to being continuously inundated with electrical, technological and other stimuli twenty-four hours a day.

Similarly, moving the body has also become distorted because so much time is spent in a sedentary position. Instead of hand washing clothes, machines are now used; instead of chopping wood and building a fire, a gas stove or a thermostat is turned on for heat.

This is not a complaint. In fact, after visiting third world countries you would probably have a deep sense of gratitude that you can push a button to heat your homes or turn a faucet to drink water. Yet it seems ironic that the once basic necessity of life, a fire in the grate, has now become a luxury.

"While living on an old wooden canal boat in my twenties, everything had to be carried at least a mile from the nearest road where I parked my car. My water, food, laundry, purchases, oil, firewood, and coal all needed to be transported to my floating home. I chopped my own wood. I tended the wood-burning stove, my only source of heat and we are speaking of English winters here! I carried, emptied and refilled the disposable toilet. Nothing happened unless my body physically executed it. My life was my exercise. As you can imagine, I was the fittest, strongest, and healthiest I have ever been. Going to the gym or running the track never crossed my mind because my lifestyle already took care of the body's physiological need for movement. Ah, but I did run, only not out of choice. The boat was moored next to a farm where there were six very angry, cantankerous geese that were worse than guard dogs. And yes, they chased me daily!" ~ Miranda

The point is, today's lifestyle can consist of many hours sitting inactive in a car, at a desk or in a chair using electric appliances or devices. Nowadays, it is vital to carve out actual time to move your body, whether this is to go hiking, practice yoga or go to the gym. This choice is imperative to your wellbeing. What is encouraged here is that, along with getting enough sleep, you physically move your body daily.

Therefore, it is essential to find a movement you enjoy, because then it will literally bring you joy. Willing yourself to do another chore that you hate will only last so long. Explore different types of movement until you find one that supports and exercises the body, but also touches and nourishes your soul. Otherwise it will become one more item on the 'to do' list.

The brilliance is, if you choose to do an activity out of a true love for yourself or because you thoroughly enjoy the movement, the energy you receive will be pure and will feed your motivation to continue.

QUEEN OF THE DANCE

"You are the universe in ecstatic motion."

~ Rumi

Dance into the sensations of your body, so much to reveal and receive.

Release all inhibitions and open yourself to where ever the movement leads.

Listen to your body.

She is your vessel, your temple, your home.

What is it she is trying to tell you?

Listen to her whispering messages.

Without thinking, where does she want to move?

Is it subtle, is it strong or is it on the inside out?

Does every part of your being desire to dance?

Receive the movement.

Allow yourself to be replenished by nature's flow.

Allow yourself to be nourished, nurtured, restored.

Release the tension built within you.

Receive the messages of your body.

Become one with the beat of your heart.

The sway of your hips, the flight of your limbs.

Let the energy that arises from the movement grow and expand from within.

Allow yourself to express who you truly are.

To become the essence of your True nature,

As she touches you, embraces you, becomes you.

Allow yourself to receive her gift living throughout your body.

Allow the sweet undulation of the breath to curl and meander through your being.

Allow the rapture of your feminine heart to flow and explore,

As you dance to the sound of mother earth.

As you beat to the drum of your own heart,

As you explore crevices and valleys of your being.

Places never touched before.

In that moment, you are free.

In that moment, you are pure beauty.

In that moment you are who you came here to be.

Claim this experience, this lesson, this deep inner guidance.

Drop into your body. Lean into her.

Become one with her.

Honor her, love her, appreciate her for housing your life force, your spirit, your soul.

Thank her for being the exquisite temple in which you live.

A space to express your bounty, your creativity, your love.

You are your body.

She is you.

Dance your dance, wherever you may be.

Dance your dance as 'You are the Queen of the Dance' said she.

WILL VERSUS WILLINGNESS

Do you will yourself through your day?
Or willingly participate in this journey called life?

Both of these words have a distinct tone and flavor to them. 'Will' tends to have a more forceful energy behind it, giving you the picture of having to push through and make your will greater than the obstacle in front of you. In contrast, **'willingly'** has a deep sense of surrender. To give willingly implies giving from the heart. Yet will is often triggered by a survival instinct, such as competitiveness or fear.

Please remember, it is not about one being better than the other is. In fact, there are times where **will** is vital, such as birthing a baby or meeting a deadline. Without will, not much is accomplished. It is all about balance. In fact, living too long in either polarity may eventually cause disease.

What is important to discern is which is most appropriate in any given moment. Is it better to **will** yourself through the traffic, weaving your way to your deadline, or to **willingly** accept the piles of cars ahead of you and call to explain why you will be late and then settle into listening to your favorite music? Each situation is different. If the latter will result in you missing a vital meeting, then the former choice will support you more.

willingness enjoys the journey.
will demands a result.
Both have power and wisdom.

"When I was travelling in Egypt I visited Mount Sinai. I was told I could walk up the ten thousand steps made by the monks or meander up the camel road that wraps the mountain in a spiral. The result would be the same. Eventually, I would reach the top where a local man would be sitting like a Buddha selling Cocoa Cola for $5.00 a bottle. Well, he had carried it up there! I knew I could will myself up those stairs. In fact, after hearing how they had been hand built, I felt a slight duty to suffer too. Alternatively, I could take my time, notice the extraordinary view on the way and walk up the trail. My will would get me up the stairs, yet my willingness would always choose the view." ~ Miranda

Just as sleeping and waking complement each other, so does balancing your will and willingness. As noted, it is about which one serves you the best in any given moment.

Interestingly, it may seem as though you have no control over your thoughts as they come streaming into your head. In fact, the first thought often seems to appear from nowhere. If left unchecked, it may continue off down its own tangent, grabbing many a supporting belief along the way. Then before you know it, you are so entangled in the web of your thoughts that to see what is really going on is next to impossible.

This can leave you at the mercy of your reactions and therefore unable to give yourself time to pause long enough to choose the best outcome. The good news is that you are able to control the second or the third thought that comes along. At any moment, you can decide to shift from a negative perspective to a positive one, change a limiting thought to an expansive one or transform will into willingness or vice versa.

*It is not always about what you are doing
which is important, but more about how you are doing it.*

willingly commit to your health.

Take a moment to think of examples in your life where you may be willing the outcome rather than choosing to be willingly present. Exercise is a wonderful expression of this. You can will yourself to the gym out of a harsh judgment, that you are...... (I will leave you to fill in the blanks here). On the other hand, you could willingly choose to move your body out of a love and tenderness for yourself, actually be present and fully live the experience.

This can greatly enhance the journey, as willingness has the ability to bring you back to the present moment. It is also less attached to the destination, and more about the adventure itself. Are these two qualities balanced in your life?

Spend A Moment To Ponder The Following:

◈ What in your life are you willingly participating in?

◈ What in your life do you will yourself to do?

EXERCISE, CHEAPER THAN THERAPY

"The shell must break before the bird can fly."
~ Tennyson

You may have noticed periods in your life that felt as though you were in the midst of a deep, long, freeze. Winter seems to have fallen causing you to hibernate. In these times, there is a strong pull to travel inward, slow down and limit all physical movement and exercise. The stagnation and lack of physical activity supports and feeds the suppression therefore limiting the possibility that physical movement might crack open the shell of your control. Even though these sluggish times may not feel good, the melancholy and depression are often stronger in their desire to keep you stuck rather than open you up.

As you lapse into winter there is no desire for the light.

No yearning for a skip or a dance. The energy is of inactivity.

Dark, heavy and persistent in its company. It is as though the creation of spring

and new growth is trapped deep below the surface of the ice and frost.

The ground is frozen hard and unforgiving.

Too constricted to allow for transformation.

Then over time, if a patient and loving hand is allowed, a crack may form.

A thaw in the cold, a slight rip in the fabric of life

where the light is able to shine through.

It may be birthed from a deep belly laugh, a sensual moment, a song or even a film.

The seed of your energy and life force, which has lain buried

and dormant under the surface of your being, awakens.

You feel a surge, a desire, a breath.

For an instant, you are freed from the shackles of winter.

There is a yearning for the light, for openness, for change.

In this moment, if you summon courage, which exists, in your heart

and say yes to the ripple on the surface of your life, the sun will shine again.

Because she is radiating light, even if eclipsed behind the shadows of your pain.

When and only when you are ready, the winter fades as the spring is born.

The dormant bud below the hard earth stirs as the ground thaws.

You rise to the surface of your existence and once again allow life force to travel

and course through your veins. It is time to be reborn again.

"It was a curious time in hindsight, the ending of a love affair as the earth fell into winter. My heart broken, my dreams dashed, my trust betrayed. My body followed suit. She slowed down, hibernated in the grief as I licked my wounds. Each week I would think I 'should' go dancing and each week I would choose isolation instead. I knew the movement, the rhythm, the beat and connection to my body would crack my depression apart. Yet it seemed I was not ready to feel fully. Spring came and I felt a stirring in my being, yet still I chose to remain closed. Then one Sunday afternoon I was invited to a meditation. It seemed innocuous enough. Sitting still, transitioning inward, I was very comfortable with that. Little did I know part of the time was free form dance. A pulsing rhythm, heart beats mixed with drum beats. Women move their beautiful bodies in sensual forms. The music and the movement cracked me back open. I could feel it. My sensuality, my sexuality, my life force being awakened from the depth of where I had buried her. She was birthed from that movement and released back into the world fully awake. It was spring and it seems I was ready." ~ Miranda

Let movement be your medicine. If you are feeling stuck, stagnant, grieving or even depressed, moving your body will cause a change. Endorphins will be released. Breath, blood, sweat and possibly tears will course through your being as you invite your temple of a body to wake up as the movement releases, transforms and sets you free. Allow movement to become your medicine. Know that you do not have to wait until spring.

Surrender to the grace of movement.

WHY EXERCISE?

"Lack of activity destroys the good condition
of every human being, while movement and methodical
physical exercise saves it and preserves it."

~Plato

Your bodies are the houses in which you live. If you do not stretch, sweat, or build muscle, these structures themselves start to break down. The human body is an extraordinary instrument and given the right tools, it will heal and align itself. The right kind of exercise is one of these vital tools.

The Physical Effects Of Exercise:

◆ Increases energy, endurance, flexibility and vitality.

◆ Helps keep you grounded and focused.

◆ Restores natural balance as the body is designed to move.

◆ Assists in maintaining an ideal weight and tones the body.

◆ Increases sexual desire and stamina.

◆ Brings more oxygen to the body and increases lung capacity, therefore supporting the respiratory system.

◆ Aids digestion and regulates elimination.

◆ Improves core strength, which leads to good posture, fewer back problems and improved skeletal muscular alignment.

◆ Increases bone density.

◆ Lowers blood pressure.

◆ Increases the 'good' cholesterol and decreases the 'bad'.

◆ Because the lymphatic system does not have its own pump, moving is the body's method to release and eliminate toxins.

◆ Improves circulation throughout the body.

◆ Allows the body to sweat, therefore releasing toxins.

The Psychological Benefits Of Exercise:

◆ Physical fitness increases your intellectual activity and capacity.

◆ Relieves stress and anxiety.

◆ Alleviates depression.

◆ Aids concentration.

◆ Clears the mind.

◆ Increases energy.

◆ Improves feelings of self-esteem, confidence, strength and power.

◆ Can unleash pent up or stored emotions from the past.

◆ Helps to process and release emotions.

◆ Elevates the mood through the release of endorphins.

◆ Can shift the nervous system from 'fight or flight' into 'rest and digest.'

The Spiritual Influences Of Exercise:

◆ Can literally lift your spirits.

◆ Helps ground the body, allowing a stable connection with your spiritual side.

◆ Can open up spiritual pathways when combined with nature or practices such as yoga or T'ai Chi.

◆ Calms the nervous system and releases the mind and body from survival mode, elevating it into the spiritual realms.

◆ Can heighten spiritual practices when consciously combined with breath.

◆ Can aid in connecting to the untapped source of feminine power and strength.

*"It is exercise alone that supports the spirits
and keeps the mind in vigor."*
~ cicero

MOVEMENT AND EXERCISE INQUIRY

Movement is a doorway to being grounded
and present in the body. From here, all things are possible.

The human body is designed to move. When you sit for hours at a desk, at a computer or in front of a television, stagnation occurs. Unfortunately, this will not only affect the physical body. Lethargy and inertia will also affect your emotions and the state of your mind. You may have noticed how a lack of movement seams to create the same influences in the other realms of your life. As the expression, 'Put your best foot forward' emphasizes, to create, manifest and make change, it is vital for a physical movement to occur. To live a fully vibrant life, it is vital to move physically the temple of the body you live in.

◈ Do you exercise daily?

◊ Yes ◊ No

◈ How many times a week do you exercise?

◈ Do you sweat?

◈ When do you prefer to exercise?

◊ Morning

◊ Afternoon

◊ Evening

◈ When do you exercise?

◊ Morning

◊ Afternoon

◊ Evening

◈ How long do you exercise for?

◈ What kind of exercises do you do?

◊ Invigorating

◊ Restorative

◊ Cardio-vascular

◊ Less demanding

◊ Mixture

◈ Does exercising give you energy?

◊ Yes   ◊ No

◈ Do you feel like you need to lie down and collapse afterwards?

◊ Yes   ◊ No

◈ Does exercise keep you at your ideal weight?

◊ Yes ◊ No

◈ Are you consistent with your exercise?

◊ Yes ◊ No

◈ Do you enjoy the exercises you are doing?

◊ Yes ◊ No

◈ Do you look forward to exercising?

◊ Yes ◊ No

◈ What exercise do you love to do?

"Those who do not find time for exercise will have to find time for illness."
~ Earl of Derby

THE WORLD OF EXERCISE

*Success can often be as simple as taking
the first single step in the right direction.*

◆ **Choose to exercise out of love for yourself.**

Use love as the motivating factor instead of the critical judge who lives in your head, who tells you more than you need to know about the shape of your body and why you should be exercising! A loving desire to nurture and take care of yourself will provide powerful fuel to your commitment to exercise and keep you motivated.

◆ **Choose an exercise that you thoroughly enjoy.**

This is vital. Yes, you might slog your way to the gym, but if, in reality, you actually love to be outside hiking, you may have noticed how, after a while, the motivation wanes. Yet if you find a movement that you enjoy and look forward to, it will be easier for you to carve out the time and keep your commitment.

◆ **When beginning a new exercise program, your muscles may become sore.**

When you start to exercise more, issues, which may have been stored in the cellular memory of the body, can be released along with toxins. Therefore, be loving and kind to yourself as you move through any transitions. Remember it is a positive outcome to release stress and toxins from either the physical, mental or the emotional bodies. As a remedy, make sure you drink plenty of water and take hot steamy showers and baths to help the body relax afterwards. Try adding a pound of Epsom salts and a pound of Baking Soda to your bath and soak for twenty minutes. This will help to relieve any exercise-induced stress to the body.

◈ **Exercise earlier in the day.**

Carve out a time first thing in the morning to move the body. As you might have noticed, if you wait until later, the rest of life seems to eat up the day. This can leave you lethargic and reluctant to get up and exercise later.

◈ **Find a partner with whom to exercise.**

This helps to make the experience more fun, holds you accountable, and provides an opportunity for mutual support and encouragement.

◈ **Join a group or a class.**

Paying in advance can certainly help your commitment. In addition, a sense of community and guidance are good changes from doing everything yourself.

◈ **Find a structured routine or rhythm.**

Walking every other weekday and going to a yoga class are good examples.

"Let us read and let us dance;
these two amusements will never do any harm to world."
~ voltaire

TYPES OF MOVEMENT

From stretching to sweating.

It is a good idea to rotate different forms of movement. This can mean a few days a week choosing exercise that is more vigorous and the other days incorporating a gentler choice. By varying your exercise program, you will use different muscle groups and promote your overall health.

Some Exercise Ideas To Incorporate Into Your Life:

◆ **GENTLE**

- ◊ Walking
- ◊ Light exercise classes
- ◊ Restorative Yoga or Pilates
- ◊ Rebounder or trampoline
- ◊ T'ai Chi
- ◊ Kegal exercises
- ◊ Household chores, yes they do count!

◆ **MODERATE**

- ◊ Hiking
- ◊ Swimming
- ◊ Dancing
- ◊ Balanced exercise classes
- ◊ Treadmill or Elliptical
- ◊ Bicycling
- ◊ Belly Dancing
- ◊ Horseback Riding
- ◊ Martial Arts, Yoga or Pilates
- ◊ Canoeing or Rowing
- ◊ Weight or Core Strength Training
- ◊ Going to the Gym

◈ INTENSE

◊ Power Walking or Running

◊ Invigorating exercise classes

◊ Hiking or Biking Up Hills

◊ Skiing or Snow Boarding

◊ Kick Boxing

◊ River Rafting

◊ Rope Courses or Rock Climbing

Movement is a vital ingredient for a vital life and is always good medicine.

MOVEMENT AND STILLNESS

Empty of doing and fill with being.

Life is made up of natural polarities. Night balances day. The birth of a child softens the death of an elder. Nature, in her infinite wisdom, will always ebb and flow and then return back to center. The miracle of this passage called life is that as human beings, you are always welcomed to follow nature's rhythm. The beauty is when you do allow yourself to be led by a more natural way of being; your body and mind will relax. A benevolent hand will guide you to love and honor yourself more.

A breakdown may occur when you choose to defy this natural synchronicity. Like a rebellious teenager you may choose to pump yourself up with caffeine or sugar and bulldoze through whatever it is that you believe is so important. Yet, it is vital not to ignore the warnings of exhaustion. By pushing through being tired instead of resting when appropriate, you will become depleted. In that moment, every message begging you to slow down and rest is disregarded. After spending so much time in motion, it is vital to drop eventually into stillness therefore regaining a sense of balance. In addition, remember, the person you are harming in this instance is you.

The trouble is, if over time you hang out too long in one extreme or another, you can become imbalanced. Eventually, the disharmony has to be addressed. Often this crash manifests itself through an accident or illness, as the pendulum will swing too far in the other direction. What is important to note here is that everything has a natural order, ebb and a flow; your breath, the moon, the tides, the seasons. It is when these rhythms are ignored that life becomes fraught and overwhelming.

"During my yoga practice, I find on days where I actively push myself further, the deliciousness of Shavasana (the resting phase) is so much deeper. It is as though all of my blood, the heat in my muscles and the depth of my breath invites in a total collapse and I succumb to a deep stillness and silence." ~ Miranda

The beauty is to invite in the flow of movement
and synchronize it with the ebb of stillness.
Allow yourself to discover this balance.

THE BREATH

change your breath, change your mind.

*H*ave you ever noticed how there are days where moving the body is effortless; in fact it flies like the wind. Hiking up a hill or walking up the stairs happens without exertion. Yet on other days, actually peeling yourself out of bed seems like too much of an effort. This phenomenon can be connected to many different conditions such as a lack of sleep, a hangover from alcohol or sugar to name a few and, yes, there are sugar hangovers! Often though, this is a sign that there is a lack of life force in the body.

This energy, also known as prana or chi, is the power supply that fuels you throughout your day. Like a battery, the human body needs to be recharged. Sleep, nourishing food, contact with nature, spirituality and laughter are a few possible ways to infuse yourself with this life force. Yet one of the most powerful and instantaneous infusions is to replenish the body through the breath.

Life force enters with the breath like a bird on the wing. As you deepen your inhale, more oxygen and energy enter the body, allowing the nervous system to relax. This softening ultimately provides more vital prana and essence to enter and can facilitate the release of toxins and stress.

By bringing consciousness to the breath, your breathing patterns can be changed.

As you alter your breathing rhythm, the body and the mind are transformed. If a situation is creating stress or fear, the breath tends to become short and shallow. By consciously taking in a few deep, long inhalations and exhalations, the pattern is changed and so is the state of the mind. The psyche is no longer connected and controlled by the fear of danger or stress. Instead, the deepening of the breath sends a clear signal to the brain that it is safe to relax.

Deep relaxed breathing and fear cannot coexist.
Just as faith and fear cannot share the same breath.

Now Take A Moment To Ponder Your Breath:

◆ Whatever state you are in right now, just pause.

◆ Do not force or change the breath.

◆ Just notice the state of your breathing.

◇ Are you breathing from the chest or the belly?

◇ Can you hardly even notice you are actually breathing?

◇ Is it shallow or deep?

◇ Is it labored or raspy?

◆ Now invite in more breath.

◇ Relax and lengthen the inhalation and the exhalation.

◇ Be careful not to strain or force too much air through your system as this may well cause stress and constrict the air passages.

◆ Soften and allow more breath and life force to enter the body.

◆ Start to breathe from the belly.

◇ Soften the muscles in the belly.

◇ Invite more breath into the inhale and release more breath on the exhale.

◇ Stay with this for a few more rounds. Take your time. There is no hurry.

◆ Soften the muscles, the tissue and even the flesh of the belly.

◆ Drop the breath down into the lower belly and the pelvic floor.

◆ Notice the state your of mind.

  ◊ Chances are, you are present, calm and possibly alert.

◆ Now go on with your day.

  ◊ Know you always have this technique available to you.

The gift of giving yourself deep, full, long breaths will provide you with more energy and an expanded state of mind.

At any moment, you can change your mind by changing your breath.

While exercising the body, the ability to receive more breath is expanded. Old toxic waste is released from the bottom of the lungs. As endurance is increased, the lungs' ability to receive more air is also amplified. This has an overall positive effect on the body. Stamina and vitality build as more life force enters.

If puffing your way up the stairs or a hill has become the norm, take heed. This is a sign that you may need activity that is more physical.

The quality of the breath is a clear message of how your physical temple is responding to any situation. It might be your body's way of suggesting that it would benefit from activity that is physical, deeper breathing and more time to relax.

DANCING KEGALS

Defy gravity.

The human body can often seem like a mystery.

Did you know that the tongue is the strongest muscle in the body and that men have nipples because all human fetus start out as girls? Well, another little-known fact is that the muscles of the pelvic floor, which run from the vagina to the rectum, are vital to your overall health and well-being.

These muscles are activated when you have to hold your pee or stop the flow. These are also the muscles needed in core strengthening exercise, such as yoga or Pilates, as they are lifted and contracted in order to stabilize the lower back. When strong, the pelvic floor can enhance sexual pleasure and lead to a more stimulating and satisfying sex life. They will also prevent you peeing involuntarily when you sneeze or cough. Need I say more?

To get a picture of this part of your body imagine a little muscular hanging hammock. Then think of pregnancy and childbirth, if this happens to have been part of your journey. Over nine months, this little hammock adjusts to carrying a much greater weight than it is used to and then, to add insult to injury, a baby is physically pushed out through a very small opening. They do not call it labor for nothing.

Even if you have not given birth, think of all the times you desperately needed to pee and waited until you actually thought you might burst. Does this sound familiar? It is highly recommend to not wait until the last possible moment, as this can put too much strain on the bladder and pelvic floor muscles. Yet worst of all, are the effects of age and gravity. As you can imagine, everything drops and unfortunately, urinary stress incontinence is not just a problem for the old and infirm. Now that a horror story has been painted, the good news is that there is a very happy conclusion.

If you do Kegal exercises daily, within a few weeks, these invisible muscles will spring back into shape. You will be pleasantly surprised when you cough, sneeze, laugh or even jump on a trampoline, as you will no longer pee involuntarily.

Practicing these simple little exercises will also help your posture and have a positive impact on all the organs these muscles hold in place.

"It wasn't until I was fooling around on a friend's trampoline that I realized there was a problem. I felt like I needed to pee so I went to the bathroom, came back and carried on jumping. A couple of minutes later I felt the need to pee again... after practicing 400 kegals a day, this is no longer an issue!" ~ Miranda

You can defy gravity even if envisioned as a serious condition or the natural force that causes things to fall to earth.

KEGAL EXERCISES

one of the simplest and most beneficial exercises you can choose to do.

There are a number of variations to this simple, yet powerfully effective exercise. The beauty is you can perform them without anyone ever knowing, you do not even have to change your clothes, shoes or shower afterwards and it only takes a moment.

Next time you are sitting at a red light, waiting in line or even having sex you can give yourself a pat on the back as you multitask through your Kegal exercises!

Repeat Any Or All Of These Exercises A Few Times A Day:

◈ **Tighten the muscles around the urethra, vagina and rectum.**

It is the same feeling as when you need to urinate and have to hold it and wait. Make sure you keep the buttocks and abdominal muscles relaxed. Over time, you can increase the amount.

◊ Hold for a count of 5.

◊ Release slowly.

◊ Repeat this 10 to 20 times.

◈ **Pulse the pelvic floor muscle up to 100 times.**

This entails lifting the pelvic floor muscle, letting it go and lifting it again before it reaches its resting position. It is done at a fast, rapid pulsing pace.

◆ This version concentrates on the rear, literally, of the pelvic floor.

　◊　Lift the sphincter muscles.

　◊　Keep lifting up between the vagina and the rectum.

　◊　Lift as high as you can go and hold for a count of 3 to 5.

　◊　Release slowly.

　◊　Repeat this 5 to 10 times a day.

◆ A more exciting approach can be to tighten the vagina during sex.

Grip as firmly as you can with your vagina while you are having intercourse and hold for a few seconds before letting go. Then wait for a reaction!

"As outlandish as this may sound, I do 400 kegals a day, the quick pulsating kind. Even on days where I am not able to exercise at least I know one area of my body is getting a work out and I didn't even have to change my clothes!" ~ Miranda

REVEAL MORE TRUTH

"Fear is what stops you...
courage is what keeps you going."
~ unknown

$\mathcal{M}$ovement is all about being in relationship with your body. As you embark upon embodying movement, please be mindful to make this journey a joyful one, not a punishment. Choose to do this out of love for yourself, not because you should.

THE FOLLOWING ARE LOVING GUIDELINES THAT WILL ENCOURAGE A NEW AND RICH RELATIONSHIP BETWEEN YOU AND YOUR BODY:

◆ **Spend some time thinking about which exercise you will actually enjoy.**
Be adventurous and try something completely different by experiencing a new form of movement.

◆ **Fill in your movement study.**

For those of you who feel this is too much like homework, please recognize that the purpose is to help you become accountable. The chart will provide insight into your patterns, and help you become accountable with your own self-care.

◆ **Please start practicing your Kegal exercises.**

Begin by doing a small amount of repetitions a few times a day. Make a note to remind yourself. A good place is in the car or where you sit for long periods of time. For example, while watching a movie, no one will know that you are completing a part of your 'Truth Work'. As your pelvic floor grows stronger, you will be able to increase the number of Kegal exercises you can do and will no longer need to cross your legs when you sneeze!

◆ **Become conscious of your breath.**

The next time you are stressed or overwhelmed, take a few deep breaths to center and align yourself. Allow this to become part of how you handle challenging situations. They say that when something has been practiced for twenty-one days it becomes part of who you are. This is a powerful tool for you to master.

◆ **Ask yourself this: 'What am I willing to do in my life?'**

This is the fundamental difference between forcing yourself to do something, rather than following your heart's desire, allowing yourself to be who you really want to be. The more you can fill your life with what you want to do, the more pleasurable the experience becomes. Begin to notice the balance between how much of your life you are willfully making happen versus willingly allowing the experience to unfold.

◆ **Start to incorporate a regular and daily movement program.**

For those of you who are already exercising and enjoy what you are doing, carry on or maybe spice it up a little by trying something new. Yet if exercise has not been part of your daily, weekly or even monthly routine, pick a movement you enjoy and simply begin. Start slowly by adding in some kind of movement two or three times a week, then build up to moving daily. This does not mean that you have to move a mountain or do hundreds of sit-ups a day. A gentle meander around the block on the first day of your period or choosing the stairs over an elevator are perfect ways to support your body.

"Every journey begins with a single step".
~ *Anonymous*

Remember that moving your body will help induce a good night's sleep and lessen food cravings. It is one of the vital components of 'The Foundational Trinity'. By choosing to live out these qualities, you will ultimately thrive.

I look forward to connecting with you again in the realms of **'Body Care'** as we explore and identify how to pamper and take care of yourself on an even deeper level.

With Love and Blessings on Embodying the Joyous Journey of Movement,

Miranda

CHARTS, CHARTS, GLORIOUS CHARTS

"Movement is the most underrated path to freedom."
~ Liz DiAlto

This Embodying Movement Study will bring a whole new level of awareness and consciousness to the vital components of movement in your life, and will give you clarity beyond measure on what is working in your world and what is not.

◆ Please go to **www.MirandaJBarrett.com/resources/embodying-movement** to print out more copies for yourself. Give yourself the gift of seeing your relationship to exercise clearly laid out in front of you.

◆ Fill out the **Embodying Movement Study** on a daily basis and you will begin to see your exercise patterns and needs, and what truly serves you.

◆ Once you are clear about your basic exercise needs and see the importance of honoring this vital aspect of your life, you can make the loving adjustments to revitalize yourself.

*"It is not who you are
that holds you back, it is who you think you are not." "*
~ Anonymous

EMBODYING MOVEMENT STUDY

DAY	Did you exercise today?	What time of day did you exercise?	What kind of movement or exercise did you do?	How long did you exercise for?	How intense was the exercise? Did you sweat?	How did you feel afterwards?	How many Kegals did you do?	What benefits did you feel after exercising?
MONDAY								
TUESDAY								
WEDNESDAY								
THURSDAY								
FRIDAY								
SATURDAY								
SUNDAY								

See your movement patterns clearly laid out in front of you.

Please go to
www.MirandaJBarrett.com/resources/embodying-movement
to print out more copies for yourself.

A RIPENING

To pause the flow of this incessant life
To stop long enough to notice the world around
To be in relationship with what is
First the damn must be built

Chop the wood
Carry the water
Blood sweat and tears

Spin the wheels
Cross the t's
Dot the i's

The faster the flow
The stronger the steal wall needs to be

Say yes to the pause
Lay claim to the stillness
Whisper loudly to the silence
Chant to Spirit
Take deeply to heart

Build the pause

Damn the torrid rapids of your mind
Let silence become the loving vice grip

To contain and hold
To ignite such a deepening
And stirring in the echoes of your soul

As to open the void
And face your demons and angels

An arising of reality
Of who you truly are

Without

Your life
Your trappings
Your trinkets

Without

Your reputation
Your tribe
Your story

Build the steel trap so strong
To capture enough of the delusion
To be stilled
And brought to the light

Let the silence remain
So pure unadulterated and infinite potential
Can partner with the fabric of the universe
And burst through the walls
Overflow the limitations
Flood the sleep state
With such a wash of awakening
That never again
Will the giant of your being
Be able to fall into such a stupor

Distill the truth
Pause your life
In order to live again

ABOUT MIRANDA
A spirited guide and mentor.

Miranda is a passionate and devoted leader. Her loving and wise support will guide you on a transformational journey as her powerful teachings unveil the truth of who you are. Her gift is to offer potent tools, which inspire exquisite and beautiful self-care and empower you to live the fullest and most authentic life possible. As a mentor and guide, Miranda deeply walks her talk and is fearless about her own path of self-discovery, as she weaves the sacred into the mundane.

The simple, yet powerful premise offered by the mystic Rumi is the foundation of Miranda's philosophy and mission:

> *"Never give from the depths of your well,*
> *always give from your overflow."*

Miranda gives Council and Guidance for the Mind, Body and Spirit. With a background in Nutrition and Energy work, Miranda is the Creator of 'A Woman's Truth' and 'The Spirit of Energy', an Author, a Workshop and Retreat Leader, a Reiki Master and Yoga and Meditation teacher. Miranda studies under the guidance of her Beloved teachers Rod Stryker and Adyashanti.

To speak with or follow Miranda, please call or visit:

Phone: 626~798~6544
eMail: Info@MirandaJBarrett.com
Website: www. MirandaJBarrett.com
Facebook: Miranda J Barrett
Twitter: MirandaJBarrett

ABOUT HELENA

A visionary artist.

Helena Nelson-Reed is a visionary artist whose primary medium is watercolor. Born in Seattle, Washington, she was raised in Marin County and Napa Valley, California and today lives in Illinois. A largely self-taught artist whose educational emphasis and degree is in psychology, Nelson-Reed's primary focus is exploring the collective consciousness and the portrayal of archetypal imagery in the tradition of Carl Jung and Joseph Campbell. Rendered in luminous watercolor technique often described as ephemeral, Nelson-Reed's paintings are created in extraordinary detail, pushing the medium of watercolor past the usual limits. Her work may be found in private collections, book covers, magazines and cd covers. Nelson-Reed also has a line of jewelry, calendars and greeting cards.

Helena's Mission:

My images can be interpreted many ways, and for some will serve as portal to the mythic landscape. Descriptions providing background about each painting are available by request. Navigating and translating myth into contemporary wisdom is the traditional way of transmitting information though a shamanic and multi-cultural practice.

Myth, fairy, folk and spiritual lore describe divine beings and supernatural life forms arriving unbidden and disguised. In our earthly dimension, mortals often play similar roles in the lives of one another. Destinies and energies collide and interact, visible and invisible forces are at work. The mythic realms are timeless, offering insight and inspiration. While my paintings have a positive energy, many have roots in the shadows of life experience and human psyche; like the lotus blossom rooted in pond mud. For many, life is one challenge followed by the next, like beads on an endless string.

Take heart! Like goddess Inanna, one may navigate the underworld, move through dark places yet return to the realms of light battle scarred but wiser, richer for the experience. Read the ancient tales, the great mythic literature; draw strength, for they are repositories of wisdom.

Visit Helena's website for her art purchase information and art to wear jewelry:

eMail: HNelsonReed@Gmail.com

Websites: www.HelenaNelsonReed.com

www.etsy.com/shop/HelenaNelsonReed

Blog: www.dancingdovestudio.blogspot.com

Facebook: MorningDove Design By Helena

MIRANDA'S WORLD

*Ways to stay connected
and aligned with your truth.*

BOOKS:

A Woman's Truth

A life truly worth living.

Priceless teachings reveal your transformational
journey ahead. Obstacles to self-care are explored
as clear and loving intentions are conceived.

The Grandeur Of Sleep

Permission to rest.

Miraculous benefits are realized as the worlds of sleep,
relaxation and rejuvenation are explored and deeply honored.

Nourishing Nutrition

Reclaim your health and vitality.

Reap the bountiful rewards while eating as nature intended.
Claim your health and vitality with these simple,
yet powerful tools to nourish and heal your body.

Embodying Movement
Ground your whole being.

Restore balance in your life. Discover how to embrace
your whole being through the life-enhancing benefits of body movement.

Body Care
Cherish your body as a temple.

Learn to honor your extraordinary body
as a living temple and listen to the healing messages she whispers.

Feminine Power
Fully access your supreme birthright.

Welcome and reclaim this intrinsic privilege while living
in harmonious balance between the masculine and the feminine.

The Abundance Of Wealth
Receive the gifts of prosperity.

Understand the energy flow of prosperity and weave
the threads of abundance throughout the tapestry of your life.

Find Your Authentic Voice

The courage to express who you truly are.

Your greatest ally is born
when you courageously speak your truth and claim your unique power.

Loving Yourself

A love affair with the self.

As you become highly attuned to your own needs,
allow love to lead the way. Grant yourself permission
to honor and express your heart's truest desires.
Love yourself, no matter what.

Living A Spiritual Life

Ground your divine essence here on earth.

Discover what spirituality means to you, by consciously
living between the two worlds of the sacred and the mundane.

Service As A Way Of Life

Ignite the fire of love to truly be of service.

By utilizing the gems of exquisite self-care
on a daily basis and honoring your truth, your mission of service is born.

The Crowning Glory
Fully Rejoice in Being You.

A celebration overflowing with love,
blessings, grace and gratitude. Stand confident within
your own truth as your mind becomes of service to your heart.

The Food of Life
The versatile vegetable.

More than just a cookbook,
a comprehensive guide for nourishing your life.

Reiki
The spirit of Energy.

An insightful guidebook full of wisdom
which introduces you to the potent and healing world of Reiki.

CARDS:

Inspiration Cards
A daily Spiritual Practice.

Sixty-Five cards with simple yet inspirational qualities
to live by and an insightful guidebook to lead the way.

CD'S:

The Grandeur of sleep and Rejuvenating Rest

An ancient healing art of rest and relaxation.

Simple yet profound practices which alleviate stress and tension allowing your mind, body and spirit to heal, restore and replenish.

TO ORDER PLEASE VISIT:

www. MirandaJBarrett.com
www.Amazon.com

*All books are available in printed or eBook form.

TESTIMONIES
to 'A Woman's Truth' teachings.

"I feel truly blessed to have experienced these amazing teachings. Miranda provides a safe and nurturing environment allowing you to go deep within yourself to both rediscover who you are, while also discovering the full potential of whom you are waiting to become. Allowing for loving space between each of the twelve books gives you the necessary time to embody fully the teachings. With each book, one after the other, you slowly begin to build upon the foundation you need to support yourself through the resurrection of who you truly are."

Dennise Marie ~ Computer Business Owner ~ San Gabriel, CA

"I hugely appreciate the variety of offerings in 'A Woman's Truth' knowing that even if I did not do all the exercises given that I can come back at any time and revisit them. I have so much more self-confidence. I now know how to do what I am here to do gratefully, with love in my heart and without resentment. Thank You!"

Barbara ~ Librarian ~ La Cañada, CA

"These books have been a graceful journey of discovering aspects of myself, reconnecting with my true inner being and have given me the tools, encouragement and permission to BE and express the powerful love of the woman that I am."

Mary ~ Business Consultant ~ Pasadena, CA

www.ingramcontent.com/pod-product-compliance
Lightning Source LLC
LaVergne TN
LVHW061229060426
835509LV00012B/1477